A
CONVENTION
OF STATES

How to Win the Battle between the Commons and the Aristocracy

DAKOTA WINDANCER

BALBOA.PRESS
A DIVISION OF HAY HOUSE

Balboa Press books may be ordered through booksellers or by contacting:

Balboa Press
A Division of Hay House
1663 Liberty Drive
Bloomington, IN 47403
www.balboapress.com
844-682-1282

Print information available on the last page.

ISBN: 979-8-7652-2934-7 (sc)
ISBN: 979-8-7652-2933-0 (e)

Balboa Press rev. date: 05/20/2022

CONTENTS

INTRODUCTION

I have not observed men's honesty to increase with their riches.
—Thomas Jefferson

The worldviews of the aristocracy are forcing many to comply or else suffer the consequences of the socialist construct of "cancel culture." Our constitutional republic is facing the greatest challenge of its time— either to remain as the supreme template of governing or to be replaced with socialistic ideologies.

America was born from the seed of desire for self-governance. That means "we the people" are the government, but somewhere along the way we seem to have forgotten our obligation to ourselves. Perhaps we trusted too much without verifying, or perhaps we allowed apathy to dictate inaction in our political affairs.

This book offers current instances that threaten our American dream of self-governance and liberties. When a government declares one set of rules for the people they are in service of and yet sets examples from another, it is time for the true government of the people to emerge with one voice, as in the days of our forefathers, in strong resistance.

The two-party system we were taught to believe in, with elected servants we can trust doing good on our behalf, is the veil of illusion that serves the aristocracy in greater ways than it could ever serve commoners such as you and me. The two-party system serving us today is the aristocracy and the rest of us.

The very institutions are hacking that for which our government was created! You are witnessing it every day in the mainstream media, press conferences, and misleading data from biased poll taking, along with the weaponization of the FBI, CDC, and NIH.

Gloom-and-doom gallops rampantly in America. Fear is both enforcer and manipulator for compliance to unconstitutional mandates and policies. People are wondering where and when this will end. The convention of states has an answer as big as the problems we face!

Article V, convention of states, was included in the Constitution for the very government we are experiencing today. Article V was written for the sole purpose of making amendments to reign in federal overreach on states, term limits, and fiscal responsibility. A thirty trillion-dollar deficit faces future generations if we do not enact a convention of states. If not now, then when?

In my first book, *A Greater Life Awaits*, I describe the king archetype as having the qualities of equanimity, constellating for his realm blessing energies and lawmaking policies that are just and fair. This fullness of royal energy spills over onto his people with blessings of support, nurturance, and the fostering of good will and unity among the people. I'd like to ask, where are America's kings today? America has been a bastion of efficacy for people around the world since its conception. Since the aristocracy and corruption of wealth has entered our forum of government, it is now time for we the people to reclaim our God-given inheritance from those who worship only themselves and the golden calf of wealth and power.

As Thomas Jefferson said, "The spirit of resistance to government is so valuable on certain occasions that I wish it always to be kept alive."

CHAPTER 1

Paradigm of Self-Governance

The brilliance of the US Constitution arose from our forefather's desire to be self-governing without the interference of a king who decided issues of commerce, trade, and law. Defeating the British was the first step in formulating America as a country. If America was to be the self-governing country our forefathers envisioned, it required a law of the land, a constitution. Deciding how to form this new constitution, was a time of bitter rivalries between the federalists and anti-federalists.

In insisting that the law of the land protect individual rights, George Mason stated boldly, "I would sooner chop off my right hand, than sign the Constitution without a Bill of Rights!"

Our freedoms are diminishing daily. We, the people, can fix what is broken. It is time for new political leaders of an old paradigm to emerge before the spirit of the Constitution is banished completely by the corruption of wealth and power and the lust of the elitists.

Foresight of the Forefathers

Could you be ready to step up and take on a leadership role with a team for a convention of states? Think of the foresight of the forefathers of our country for a moment.

John Jay, who became our first Supreme Court Justice, is quoted as saying, "No power on earth has a right to take our property from us without our consent."

James Madison—who served as a colonel in Virginia's fourth militia and later became our fourth president—is quoted as saying, "If tyranny and oppression come to this land, it will be in the guise as a foreign enemy."

Alexander Hamilton served as an assemblyman in the New York legislature and as a lieutenant colonel during the revolution, and later became the new nation's first secretary of the treasury. Hamilton is quoted as saying, "Those who stand for nothing, fall for everything."

What these men have in common is that they were regular guys who saw that true patriots must take a stand for liberty. Together, they drafted the *Federalist Papers*, which resulted in the ratification of the original Constitution. Throughout the essays of the *Federalist Papers*, each of these men warned of the nature of man's propensity to court the energies of greed, power, and lust.

We read these warnings today for their prophetic insight. The Constitution was painstakingly drafted to include the Bill of Rights and Article V as a safeguard against a tyrannical government. Our forefathers wanted us, the people, to have the last say in how we are governed, and through Article V of the Constitution, they left us a way of preserving that noble intention. It is now time for us as American patriots to become the like-minded statesmen that America desperately needs. Now more than ever it is our time to step up and model for our servant leaders the virtues of prudence, justice, fortitude, and temperance.

We can emulate good diplomacy and put our faith into action by calling for a convention of states. The unifying cause of the commoner must be to *cancel the aristocracy* that is robbing us of our liberty and justice.

Shining as We Should

Citizens are proving daily that we will stand up, speak up, and show up to keep our liberty! We are a citizenry of powerful and passionate people invested in and paying more than lip service to the sociopolitical affairs and capabilities of our fine state.

The volunteer works of Florida's Convention of States Action has been so effective that the opposition is rearing its head in the attempt to rescind Florida's 2014 application for a convention of states. Now is our time to shine as we should—not playing small or shrinking in the face of threat but manifesting the glory of God within us and standing firm with faith in action! Convention of States is an insult to the factions of the aristocracy that want a larger, more centralized government that gets to decide what is best for you and me.

Can you see with the eyes of your heart that together in one formidable mass of unity, we can set off a political sequence comparable to the first shot heard around the world? These moments are why we patriots signed the petition and become volunteers. These are the moments that will define our resolve and leadership.

Many in number, with smiles on our faces and hymns in our hearts, let us model political eloquence by showing up fully confident that we as the majority shall not shrink—we happily answer the call to our personal hero's journey and that of affecting the future generations. In so doing, we emulate and replicate our forefathers' spirits and intentions while they made the thirteen colonies into one great nation.

We are already patriots; we now can elevate ourselves to statesmen!

Homeostasis for America

The problem with Socialism is that you eventually
run out of other people's money.
—Margaret Thatcher

Socialism has never failed because it has never been tried.
—Anti-capitalists

Our objective world is becoming increasingly complicated and often pits the "isms" of one social construct (capitalism) against another (socialism). Here are some observations that may be of interest and help elucidate the matters of choice and decision that make a government viable.

The wave of the Great Reset promises through the altruistic lens of progressivism that it is time to eliminate racism, fascism, and economic inequality. This paradigm is being marketed as distinctive in solving the ills of American inequality and consumer addiction to fossil fuel. Progressives wish to formulate and promote public policies based on the premise that the state is wise, and the market is stupid.

According to an article published by the Heritage Foundation, after World War II, India, Israel, and Great Britain adopted socialism as an economic model and failed. Progressive attacks on capitalism had been key to putting Hitler into power.

Democratic socialists want their form of government to define freedom for us. The analogy offered is that it is better to live as a shop manager on meager resources than be labeled and liquidated as the bourgeoisie with conventional attitudes. The fatal conceit of socialism is that its system can make better decisions for the people than they can for themselves. The fact is that socialism has failed in every country it has been tried. The argument that China, Russia, and the Netherlands are socialist is simply not true. These countries are an amalgam of capitalist, socialist, and communist ideologies.

Does this analysis of socialism mean that capitalism is without its own shadows? Absolutely not! We must, however, evaluate *radical* and *new* in term of whether it is wise or unwise.

The four guiding principles of capitalism are higher purpose, stake owner orientation, conscious leadership, and conscious culture.

Capitalism exists for profit not only monetarily but in the areas of efficient production, financial incentives, and efficient allocation of resources. It has a built-in mechanism for overcoming discrimination and bringing people together. Economic freedom helps political freedom. Capitalism allows for private property rights, free markets, and competition. Capitalism has propelled innovation and prosperity in modern society.

Through the sovereign use of capitalism, America gives more money in foreign aid than any country in the world. As an example, the US Agency for International Development (USAID) has nearly $10 billion in emergency relief set aside for COVID-19 distribution, not including millions of US dollars for international infrastructure and other programs abroad.

The shadows of capitalism are found in:

- monopoly power
- inequality, creating social division
- boom and bust cycles
- diminishing marginal utility of wealth
- ignoring social benefit

As you can see, neither ism supplies the utopian world that most of us would relish living in. The question is, Is the ism at fault, or is it the propensity of human beings who can't seem to help themselves from exploiting opportunity for selfish gain?

In the final analysis, after looking at the pros and cons of each, I believe it is imperative to distinguish between the premises of each economic construct and to ask yourself a question. Do you want a nationalism that preserves independence, freedom, rugged individuality, and equal opportunity (and perhaps not equal outcome), or an alternative nationalism under a government that defines pretty much everything for you?

Our forefathers knew that men would find a way to corrupt even the kingdom of heaven with their proclivity for power, lust, greed, and indolence. Capitalism without virtue and expedience is what needs fixing. Fault is never in the ism, but in the management of it.

Imposing term limits within our republican government is one way to prevent bad policy from being passed into law and to remove those who work against constitutional principles. Socialists rant against fascism and inequality, but their policies are paving the way for it! There is no guarantee of success in anything. No matter your level of talent, work ethic, or skill, failure runs parallel to success. Capitalism gives everyone an opportunity to compete at any level, rewarding ingenuity, innovation, and resolve to succeed without college degree or high position. Many of today's most influential people are proof of that—Mark Zuckerberg, Bill Gates, and the late Steve Jobs, to name only a few! Where would these men be without the capitalist paradigm? Working for the state at a meager wage?

Governor Ron DeSantis's decision not to comply with another lockdown in the state of Florida has allowed businesses to reap revenues lost during the previous lockdown. He has shown that Florida fared better in COVID-19 related cases than many of the states choosing to mask up and lock down. It seems that the more the Governor does what is right for the people of Florida, the bigger the target he becomes for those who wish to implement stringent restrictions under the guise of general welfare and public safety.

United effort builds better societies. This is how the commoner defeats the tyranny of the aristocracy.

CHAPTER 2

Reframing Reality

Technology today is manipulating our daily reality. Realities are reframed as conspiracy theory and lies become the truth very easily when they cannot be challenged or, more devastatingly, are not being challenged. We know *less* about our world today because it is hidden from us through media manipulation, political agendas, apathy, and lethargy.

Media wizards of today know that power depends on people creating and believing in fictions. Misinformation is the tool of the shadow manipulator who shows up at press conferences to give just enough information to incite strong emotional reaction in people but fails to give all the relevant facts for intelligent reasoning and appropriate action.

When ceremonies and celebrations are limited and speech is edited by politically correct standards, authentic communication wanes, and soon the fear of being canceled by corporations and tyrannical overseers makes dialogue difficult. As a result, the individual abdicates the right of free speech. Limiting words is the limiting of thought, and that is not what our forefathers intended for governing.

Defining the Shadow Government

> Throughout history the rich and the aristocracy
> always imagined they had skills superior to everybody
> else's, which is why they were in control.
> —Yuval Noah Harari

In his book *21 Lessons for the 21ˢᵗ Century,* Harari shares his assessment and fallen state of the human family: "Individual humans know embarrassingly little about the world, and as history has progressed, they have come to know less and less."

Those things that are hidden, repressed, or denied are shadows. Things we do not know about, or things withheld, are shadows as well, and that is the subject at hand.

Most voters ascribe to the false belief that the two-party system is composed of Democrats and Republicans. But they are not the main players—they are merely the stage props artfully planted by the aristocracy. While the professional working class grows contentious about left and right policies, from their insulated fortress installed high above any fray the aristocracy watches how well their money is working for them, dividing the people by class, race, and gender.

The financial resources of the aristocracy need to be minimized through term limits. Term limits is the best way to keep business out of government, and government out of our business. Term limits within our federal government will give a voice back to the people in terms of how we want our government to operate and will restore amicability within that government by exponentially downsizing aristocratic influences.

We as a people are being divided by the psychological projections of an aristocratic worldview. Making enemies of everything is good for their business of deconstructing our democratic republic or any other government they wish to topple for their own power lust.

Citizens are standing strong in their resolve to see responsible government return to the White House, Senate, and House of Representatives. The mission of each citizen to act, learn, and adapt helps to remove the veils of shadow manipulation. By reaching, teaching, and activating others, we foster a freer society and ensure the welfare of future generations.

As you can see, "shadow government" is not a term from a conspiracy theory (another projection from the aristocratic worldview) nor a mystical term for a nonexistent mythical force. To use the term *Shadow Government* is simply to place the focus on the puppet masters of shadow manipulation through the censorship of mainstream media and social media (such as Twitter, Amazon, and Facebook) that regulates the flow of content. Shadow government, if you haven't surmised it by now, is the aristocracy that uses its wealth to subvert cause and effect. Aristocracy has always been the creator of most of the world's troubles. Aristocracy acts much like a toddler pounding on the highchair tray demanding "More!"

The Convention of States (COS) is shining light where the shadow lurks by educating those who don't know about Article V. When enough people around the nation are properly informed about self-governance and what that means, the days of shadow manipulations will grow shorter. It is our responsibility to know more about the world instead of less and less. Harari has pointed out the problem, and COS is a great component for the solution.

What has made American society so great has been its response in overcoming adversity. We must act as Americans who stand for America and no longer be the unsuspecting agents of divisiveness on behalf of the aristocracy, who will always eat at the banquet table while the rest of the world scrambles for the falling crumbs.

Decide now! Do you want a voice in the ruling class, as was designed by our Constitution, or would you rather shrivel on the vine of existence as your liberty, freedoms, and happiness are daily taken away from you?

This question illuminates the battle between the commoner and the aristocracy.

Complicating the Constitution

In his pamphlet *Common Sense,* Thomas Paine makes the important distinction between society and government:

> Society is produced by our wants, and government by wickedness; the former promotes our happiness positively by uniting our affections, the latter negatively by restraining our vices. The one encourages intercourse, the other creates distinctions. The first is a patron, the last a punisher.

I would like to share a perspective formulated by observation and historical fact, then invite you to simmer in some questions I raise.

It is no secret that our Constitution is under attack. These judgments include that it was composed by racists, is arcane in today's political climate, and has been rendered obsolete. Attacking the Constitution, making it seem exceedingly complex, keeps the solution of societal ills at bay without discovering in which part the fault lies—some say in one, and some in another, with every political physician advising different medicine. Do we see that today?

Repeating specious content through media marketing and through the voice of opposition to our beloved Constitution allows time to make more converts than reason. Are we seeing that today?

The question must be asked, when constitutional principles are being weaponized against the very people the Constitution was written to protect, whose interest is being served? Isn't that federal overreach?

When an attempt is made to reframe the general welfare clause to turn ordinary citizens into domestic terrorists for not ascribing to vaccine passports or embracing the ideology of current administration, again it must be asked, whom is that serving? How does that political perspective uphold life, liberty, and the pursuit of happiness? Is this a component of federal overreach?

We face three choices in making the legal voice of the people heard: a convention of states, military power, or a mob.

It seems to me that a convention of states is the best of the three ways to remain a sovereign nation.

Is it federal overreach when elected officials put the Constitution on trial rather than upholding it? Do they not take an oath and swear to uphold and defend the Constitution?

Could attacking the Constitution be a clever guise to avert attention from a lack of personal integrity and virtue?

Might it be true that the simpler we make government, the less liable it is to be disordered? Wouldn't it be easier to repair when it became disordered?

Is it any wonder that more people than ever are flocking to the Sunshine State? Floridians are fortunate in having a governor who upholds freedom of choice, while local confederations and school boards enabled by the federal government work to take that freedom from us by weaponizing fear and party agendas.

I have shared my concerns and a perspective on how the usurpation of our Constitution continues and will most likely broaden. As American patriots, we are being called to action. Will you answer the call to stand in the battle against the aristocracy that wants to rule over us, or will you hit the snooze alarm?

Your decision may decide the fate of the nation you live in—for better or worse.

Politically Correct Speech:
A Pandora's box for Lawmaking

Enumerated powers were included by the framers of our Constitution for the sole purpose of limiting government overreach and for providing checks and balance among the executive, judiciary, and legislative branches.

James Madison declared in *Federalist* 45 that "the powers delegated by the proposed Constitution to the federal government are few and defined."

The Supreme Court will soon be deciding the case of *Cummings v. Premier Rehab Keller,* which, after all the legal context is diluted, becomes a legal case for the right to sue entities based on emotional distress—otherwise known as *feelings.* What should be of concern to all of us is the potential legal precedent this may set for future rulings, and the threat to religious liberties.

According to an article in *The Daily Signal,* the Supreme Court has previously never articulated whether compensatory damages include emotional distress. While this case has flown under the radar, it will have colossal implications for the ongoing legal battle to protect religious freedom, especially as it intersects with modern interpretations of civil rights law and governmental anti-discrimination provisions.

The ramifications of the Supreme Court's decision in *Cummings v. Premier Rehab Keller* will extend far beyond disability law. Emotional distress is entirely subjective and could be used as a pretext to sue people and businesses under anti-discrimination law when the only alleged discriminatory conduct involved is honoring one's religious beliefs. If Premier Rehab is forced to pay emotional distress damages to Cummings, what of the medical practitioners who refuse to perform mastectomies on transgender patients or bakeries that decline to make custom cakes for same-sex couples? Do you see the potential damage that awaits small business owners?

In reading this article in *The Daily Signal*, I began to wonder how much of all this legal wrangling was presented into the judiciary establishment by its precursor of politically correct speech? While teaching at a well-known university in the 1990s, I was told by the Dean that to retain my position as an associate lecturer, I must eliminate the use of the words "men," "women," "boys", or "girls" because they were not gender neutral. Now, thanks to the exploitation of the general welfare clause and a conscious ignoring of enumerated powers, woke ideologies are becoming the status quo in federal proceedings—not just on liberal college campuses.

Folks, the writing is on the wall for our republic. A bloated and larger government is making decisions for us based on new legal precedents and by reframing the intended definitions of "enumerated powers" and "general welfare." Politically correct speech has opened a Pandora's box of not hurting other people's feelings, so that they can sue us if we do. Since when is the government legally responsible for the way I feel? Isn't that a private issue that provides fertile ground for personal growth? Where would this type of legal wrangling ever end? Feelings are a personal experience of perception, too subjective to be considered as a legal basis. "You hurt my feelings! For not liking me, I'm going to sue you!"

The government now wants to do our thinking and growing up for us. To this I say, "No thanks! I would rather call for a convention of states that will write new amendments limiting your interference in my and our living expressions."

Due Diligence of a Good Warrior

Ever since humans became conscious of their ability to subdue the earth, the pernicious effects of lust for power have become the black hole that warps the space around it. In *21 lessons for the 21ˢᵗ Century, Yuval Noah Harari* makes this statement:

> Great power inevitably distorts truth. Power is all about changing reality ... When you have a hammer in your hand, everything looks like a nail; when you have great power in your hand, everything looks like an invitation to meddle.

Victories obtained against larger opponents in any battle must start first with differentiating exactly who the enemy is. The three qualities of a good warrior are *dualizing* (black or white), *differentiating* (recognizing and ascertaining), and *identifying* (establishing and indicating).

The greatest enemy we are facing today is not found in any political party. Technocracy is the modern aristocracy that today meddles in the affairs of the professional worker and everyday American. The elite of technical experts have bought their way into governments upon this entire planet.

The war we must wage in our mutual passion to save the republic must not be waged within the party lines of left or right but by not allowing, for example, people who know nothing about meteorology or biology to propose policies regarding climate change and genetically modified crops. *Differentiating* between political party and technocracy is part of the due diligence of good warrior work. *Identifying* the true enemy as technocrats versus party saves valuable time and resources. *Dualizing* our attack after identifying who the true enemy is gives us a keen sense of how to fulfill the mission for victory. But how do we do this in a practical manner, and not just theoretically?

The key to defeating the larger enemy of technocracy is through limiting the terms of office of those who have made backdoor alliances with the meddlesome power players. We must cut the legs off the game table of technocracy by acting as able and fit warriors, learning every day another way to combat righteously what does not serve us, and we must adapt our attacks so as not to be predictable or recognizable to our enemies. We must use the brilliant simplicity of our Constitution with sophistication in applying all its built-in safety features.

The fullest expression of warrior energy serves to preserve life, not take it. The warrior serves as the agent who provides safety and protection under a sovereign government. Floridians, as an example, are fortunate that the fullest positive pole of warrior energy is embraced by a majority. This example is reflected in the people's overwhelming support of their past and current governor. Floridians, by majority, vote for their sovereignty of state and do not wish to toe the line for federal mandates they see as damaging and unfair.

We must stop wasting time with useless arguments against the wrong enemy set up by the smokescreens of the ruling technocracy class. Convention of States Action (COSA) provides us with the weapons for defeating the larger opponent of technocracy, not allowing its clandestine agents to get comfortable in office for very long.

As iron sharpens iron, so must liberty-loving warriors sharpen their swords.

CHAPTER 3

State Sovereignty

If it were not for men like Patrick Henry and George Mason, the Tenth Amendment may never have been written into the Constitution that gave us the Bill of Rights and individual state sovereignty.

Article 1, Section 8, of the Tenth Amendment holds that all rights and powers not specifically reserved by Congress are reserved by either the states themselves or by the people. The Constitution may never have been ratified by its framers if this insistence on the Bill of Rights and state sovereignty had not been added. Today these stipulations stand between being governed through dictatorship or remaining a constitutional republic of the people.

Political Passion, Alive and Well

The American literature professor Joseph Campbell, whose work covered many aspects of the human experience, more than once stated that "the privilege of a lifetime is being who you are." The privilege provided by the Collier County Republican Executive Committee Meeting, held October 4,2021 in Naples, Florida, did not disappoint in terms of authenticity, contention, and passionate sharing of political perspectives. Heated passion began when the attending members were trying to decide whether the discussion of item 11, a convention of states, should be included in the agenda.

Byron Lowell Donalds, representative for Florida's Nineteenth district, was in attendance. His district serves the heart of Southwest Florida, including Cape Coral, Fort Myers, and Naples. approximately two hundred concerned members and citizenry also attended, and many motions were proposed and carried.

A motion was made and voted that item 11, convention of states, be removed from the agenda. This was a win for COS and hardworking volunteers, as the opposition in favor of rescinding the application had no traction.

I felt a swelling pride rising within my heart and throat as I listened to the utter sincerity and authentic concerns expressed so articulately and passionately by several attending members. It was, indeed, an inspiring experience to witness the fervency and powerful voice from many patriotic women and men.

Perspectives are of course a very relative element for interpreting reality and have the risk of being flawed. However, here goes mine …

That night's meeting held abundant gold for my wife and me. We were moved by the strength and power of the committee board members for holding the chairperson accountable to following the necessary protocols that keep meetings on point and more importantly safe for all members in equal sharing. It was apparent to me that the women of the board were invested in the issues, ailments, and solutions, while the men wrestled with personality conflicts.

There was ample time given for various candidates to speak and explain their positions on assorted topics. Decorum took up residence during this section of the meeting, and the candidates rendered a good account of themselves.

I find it difficult to end my assessment without saying how proud it makes me feel to see the passion for American ideals expressed so well by my Floridian brothers and sisters. I am a close neighbor of formidable folk who exhibit knowledge, power, and passion, and I count myself fortunate to be a part of that shining citizenry.

Governor DeSantis Understands His Duty in Our Constitutional Republic

For every problem there is a solution, and while the mainstream media report falsely that a driver shortage is the cause for goods not delivered, Florida's governor knows better. Governor DeSantis mirrors the voice of the people and has become the paladin of our turbulent times acting on behalf of not only Floridians but for the workers of America. Governor DeSantis has extended an open invitation for the cargo ships to make Florida their docking destination. Working with Michael Rubin, president, and CEO of the Florida Ports Council, he has announced that "Florida is open for business and is the solution in resolving the global supply chain crisis."

While DeSantis's policies are fostering a working America and nurtures the state economy by resisting a host of mandates sent down from the White House, they in turn become the affecters of American ideals and constitutional living. We the people of Florida are enduring the stormy weather of political jousting because our governor does not sleep on his watch! While some parts of our government work to undermine the inalienable rights of its citizenry, the paladin of Florida champions those causes with righteous temerity.

The federal overreach of the White House does not prevail in Florida as it does in other states because Governor DeSantis uses his influence for fostering, affecting, and nurturing economic and general health for all Floridians. Florida is at the time of this writing among the states with the lowest rate of COVID-19 infection, to give one example.

Isn't it alarming to you that the states that are languishing are led by the negative influences of authoritarianism, censorship, and propaganda ministries? America is in a midlife crisis: republic or socialist state? Keep in mind that socialism has failed everywhere it has been tried.

While some wish to sever the bonds of kinship with our forefathers and surrender to the woke and progressive ideology of Karl Marx, many of us are bonded to Patrick Henry's words: "Give me liberty *or* give me death!"

From the experience of our personal world-building we know the words of Ben Franklin to be true:

> "Nothing can stop the man with the right mental attitude from achieving his goal; nothing on earth can help the man with the wrong mental attitude, energy and persistence conquers all things."

Governor DeSantis understands the words of James Madison when he said, "Ambition must be made to counteract ambition, the advancement and diffusion of knowledge is the only guardian of true liberty." We the people are the only legitimate fountain of power, according to Madison. If we believe that in any measure, then we also must act!

We can mitigate the nation's midlife crisis and growing pains when we act, coming together as Americans in unified action to preserve life, liberty, and the pursuit of happiness. What nobler cause is there than the commoner confounding the cause of aristocratic manipulation?

As Thomas Jefferson said, "Do you want to know who you are? Do not ask, act! Action will delineate and define you."

Speaking Truth to Power

Children do not have any voice regarding federal or local policy making, yet they are subject to its ill effects just as they are to the positive. So, who will speak for the voiceless?

Kelly Robbins, who lives in Ocala, Florida, is an Air Force veteran, self-employed medical professional, and volunteer for the Convention of States Action. I met Kelly, and she is taking the COSA tenets to *reach, teach,* and *activate* not only to heart but directly to the board of education in her local community. Kelly's concerns are children's health and the federal and local overreach in enabling and enforcing what many feel is bad policy. Her motivation stems from "getting local and getting involved."

Kelly receives support from her regional captain, Coach Thomas, and is "on fire" to be a voice who speaks on behalf of elementary children forced to wear masks throughout the school day. *Life Site News* lists forty-seven studies confirming the ineffectiveness of masks for COVID and thirty-two more confirming their negative health effects. The overreach of government lies in the fact that the science regarding immunity is being manipulated and reframed by the CDC and the media. Further cases of federal overreach are evidenced recently by the president's stand against Governor DeSantis's executive order of no mask mandates. Governor DeSantis has threatened to withhold pay from local school boards who are choosing to defy this order, while the president has stated he will neutralize that action by providing funds ... somehow!

These mandates brings into question not only government overreach in our education system but the efficacy of fiscal responsibility. Our nation is 30 trillion dollars in debt. The US Senate passed another trillion-dollar infrastructure bill and now may pay off local school boards with borrowed money we do not have.

In these dire times, Kelly has spoke her "truth to power" to the school board in Ocala on September 14,2021 This event was livestreamed on YouTube. As you can see, this event had many facets. It addresses health risks of children, the enabling of bad policy by local school boards through federal support, and the diminishing right of freedom to choose. Why is it asking too much for parents to decide the way their children are raised and where the responsibility of federal government begins and ends in doing so?

Superheroes do not require capes or costumes to affect change—they need only to speak their truth to power and act!

The reason the Convention of States exists is to provide a solution to the issues of government overreach, fiscal responsibility, and term limits. When commoners act in unity, the aristocrats call for a negotiation of terms. It is in these events that we truly discover that our truth does have power!

Dakota Windancer

Protecting the Rights of Unvaccinated Workers

Florida lawmakers have introduced two bills, SB 4B and HB 3B, to protect employees who refuse to be vaccinated from being terminated. Under these new bills, employers who enforce Biden's unconstitutional vaccination mandates on their employees face a fine of $10,000–$50,000 for each offense.

The opposition to these bills is crying foul because these bills require no public disclosure. The opposition fears businesses may receive more favorable treatment while others may be aggressively prosecuted (https://www.tampabay.com/news/florida-politics/2021/11/15/florida-lawmakers-push-records-exemption-to-protect-unvaccinated-employees). Welcome to the ever-expanding frontier of American politics.

The larger and more prominent issue of forced vaccination, which is *not* an enumerated power of federal government, is being pushed to the back of line, while accusation without proof by the opposition race to the forefront.

What about the right of privacy? If the opposition fears favorable treatment on the one hand and aggressive prosecution on the other, where is their concern for the individual who risk losing their jobs by living their beliefs and values?

Wouldn't it be nice if lawmakers from both sides of the aisle would embrace collectively the bigger picture of constitutional efficacy for its citizenry? Partisanship is the new occult in today's political arena. It has become more important for lawmakers to find fault and tear down than it is to work toward a consensus and to build up. Florida is a state that is attracting new residents at an alarming pace. I wonder if it has anything to do with the policy making that protects its citizenry against federal overreach? When servants of government put partisanship ahead of their constituency and the general welfare, it is time to limit their participation it that government. As George Mason said, "Considering the natural lust for power so inherent in man, I fear the thirst of power will prevail to oppress the people."

Our forefathers always intended that there be a continuous rotation of public servants within our government. With the activation of an Article V convention of states, we the people can have a say in new amendment making and rescind the lifestyle of career politicians and judges!

Florida remains steadfast in her sovereignty, but that is being threatened by partisanship and party agendas. We as voters must educate ourselves more about the government we have, and the government we want. George Mason makes clear his vision for government:

> "Government is, or ought to be, instituted for the common benefit and security of the people, nation, or community; whenever any government shall be found inadequate or contrary to these purposes, a majority of the community hath indubitable. unalienable, indefeasible right, to reform, alter, or abolish it, in such manner as shall be judged most conducive to the public Weal."

Let this be our call to action to let our legislators know what kind of government we want and what our expectation is of them for providing it.

CHAPTER 4

Aristocrats versus Commoners

The greatest threat to a sovereign government is found within the people who take part in it. Contained within the essays of the *Federalist Papers*, written by Alexander Hamilton, John Jay, and James Madison, the prophetic warning of greed, power lust, and use of office for the exploitation of trade and commerce was made abundantly clear. When money drives the machine, only those with vast resources of money will become the overlords of society. To get the government out of our business, we must get business out of our government!

More than two-thirds of sitting members of Congress are receiving checks that amount to $11 million in campaign giving, and 356 lawmakers have received checks from the biggest drug makers.

Aristocrats are subverting society with cancel culture tactics, influencing lawmakers with campaign donations and watching the chaos and decline of an ordered society from behind the guarded walls of their personal empires, built on the backs of the commoners' efforts. We are now experiencing the government our forefathers warned us about!

The Aristocrats Are in Charge

At the time of this writing, Pfizer, BioNTech, and Moderna are earning a combined rate of $65,000 in profit *every minute* for their vaccines, according to the Peoples Vaccine Alliance.

We the people not only are suffering the effects of forced masking along with the alpha, delta, and omicron variants of COVID-19 but are literally being used to drive up profit margins for these Big Pharma companies!

Let us also take into consideration other supplemental drugs being sold for the treatment of symptoms acquired by many Americans after receiving the jabs. My wife, as an example, contracted idiopathic urticaria and has been seeing a specialist for months toresolve this ailment. So far, the steroid prednisone is all that helps in relieving her symptoms but is in no way a viable treatment.

Furthermore, the term "idiopathic" means that it is of unknown origin! Interesting and startling, isn't it? My wife and I both are left wondering how many other Americans are experiencing various side effects after receiving the jab, left unreported because "idiopathic" makes the proving ground exceedingly difficult, since origins are untraceable. I find it interesting too that these companies have sold most doses to rich countries, leaving low-income countries out in the cold.

I wish to be truly clear: I am and always will be a strong advocate for freedom of choice. Mandates for the military and yesterday's heroes working in the medical profession are irresponsible, negligent, and unconstitutional. In my view, they are crimes against humanity comparable to the gas chambers of Auschwitz.

Every American should wish to rid America from its aristocracies of Big Pharma, Big Tech, and the ruling class in Washington that works only to remain in office. It is time for us not to rely on the expertise of those who are part of the cabal of corruption. Our reliance on bought and paid for groupthink may become the reason for the fall of what remains of our republic and our own personal health!

We still have the chance to cancel the aristocracy running our government. We can neutralize the minions of corrupt policy making by calling for the first-ever Article V convention of states. A convention of states has the power to propose constitutional amendments that limit the size and scope of the federal government. These amendments can decentralize power away from Washington, making it much more difficult for big companies to lobby for the legislation they want. *This is the government our forefathers warned us about.* The dilemmas we face today are the reason the signers of the Constitution added the Bill of Rights and Article V.

Article V provides an opportunity for adding term limits, federal fiscal responsibility, and federal overreach as amendments to our Constitution. Fixing what is wrong with American politics and leadership within our republic is not up to our elected officials; it is up to the citizenry—you and I coming together collectively as *we*, "We the People in order to form a perfect union."

We are at the crossroads of America's survival as a constitutional republic. This is the time for each of us to answer the call to our hero's journey. Hitting the snooze alarm may negate any chance in our future.

Are you beginning to see clearly now the battle front and the psychological warfare waged between the commoner and the aristocracy?

Ancient Roman Aristocrats and the Biden Elite

The natural progress of things is for liberty to
yield, and government to gain ground.
—Thomas Jefferson

QUESTION: What do the aristocracy of ancient Rome and the modern world have in common? ANSWER: The litters they ride upon are carried on the backs of everyday American citizens.

The elitists love their pageantry and displays of altruism among the masses. The latest display occurred in Rome, Italy, during a weekend when I was writing this book. Can you see the metaphor here?

A motorcade of eighty-five limousines winding through the streets of Rome carrying our president doesn't seem to "count" toward the carbon emissions that were to be discussed at Sunday's COP26 UN Climate Change Conference. Biden's climate envoy, John Kerry, has already put 138 metric tons of carbon in the air using his private jet. Emissions calculator and flight data indicate that he alone has emitted thirty times the amount of carbon emitted by a typical passenger vehicle per year. And this data was collected only between January 10 to August 6 2021.

The jeweled poles of the aristocracy's "litter" that we carry come in the form of regulations and restrictions that our elected servants thumb their noses at. "This for the betterment of humanity," they say. Rules for thee, but not for me is the actuality.

Americans and people around the world need to realize soon that the elitists' virtue signaling is used to subjugate the masses through the guise of cleaner energy and vaccine mandates. If these high-minded servants of the common people are concerned with climate change, as they claim, then why not use Skype, video calls, or Zoom? After all, much of America's business is done this way by the everyday citizen.

But as Thomas Jefferson stated, "I have not observed men's honesty to increase with their riches." Indeed, we are taxed to fund electric cars that increase their riches.

I ask why China and India are not held accountable in this concern for climate change. They are the two largest countries creating the most carbon emissions.

In any disagreement, agreements can be attained, but they must be based on the principles of honesty, integrity, and accountability. Our forefathers proved this trying to form a country while fighting the British. The wisdom distilled from disagreement came in the form of Article V of the US Constitution. The convention of states gives us the power to make new amendments for addressing term limits, responsible fiscal spending, and the overreach of our federal government. As patriotic Americans, we would do well in adapting the same attitude as Samuel Adams during the struggle for independence:

> "If ye love wealth better than liberty, the tranquility of servitude better than the animating contest of freedom, go home from us in peace. We ask not your counsels or your arms. Crouch down and lick the hands which feed you. May your chains set lightly upon you, and may posterity forget that you were our countrymen"!

Desire is the ingredient needed for achieving this monumental undertaking. Do you desire a free America for your children and their children's children?

We must remember, "We are not the *servants,* but the *master."*

The Infrastructure Bill Is Not about Infrastructure

> This is the tendency of all human governments. A departure
> from principle becomes a precedent for a second; that second
> for a third; and so on, till the bulk of society is reduced to mere
> automatons of misery, to have no sensibilities left but for sinning and
> suffering ... And the fore horse of this frightful team is public debt.
> Taxation follows that, and in its train wretchedness and oppression.
> —Thomas Jefferson

According to an article in *Fortune* magazine, the 1.2 trillion-dollar infrastructure bill is only a precursor to a larger multiple-trillion-dollar bill that has moderates on both sides unhappy and the radical elements of Congress licking their chops for passage.

Some Democrats are claiming that the bill will pay for itself through a multitude of measures and without raising taxes. But the Congressional Budget Office brushed aside several of those paid-for provisions that would add billions more to the deficit over the next ten years.

In the final tally, the infrastructure part of this more than 1,200-page bill accounts for only 30 percent of a proposed $2.65 trillion plan announced by the White House. This analysis comes from CNN fact-checking.

John Marshall, a founding father and the fourth Chief Justice of the Supreme Court, said "The power to tax is the power to destroy." As income rises, it is taxed at a higher rate, and the last dollar an American earns is taxed more than the first dollar. This is known as a progressive tax system. Hmm ... sound complicated? It is. Tax codes and tax rates are scary enough, but it is what is hidden in the follow-up bill that should give us pause and cause us to reflect.

Jefferson observed that the departure from principle becomes a precedent for the second, third, and so on departure, until the bulk of society is reduced to automatons of misery. We *are* entering into that stark and potential reality!

When the House sent this bill to Biden for his signature, they may have opened a door for further precedents that will burden the citizenry of America. Do we need an infrastructure bill? Absolutely we do! But not at the cost of a larger Democratic social spending plan. With the deficit already at $30 trillion, we must ask whether spending trillions more is prudent or fiscally responsible, especially where unspecified enhancers may be hidden within the bill, those taxpayers will foot the bill for and not be in agreement.

If only 30 percent of the current bill pertains to actual infrastructure, what is in the other 70 percent?

Furthermore, after this precursor, how many more precedents will we the people have to accept from a government with dangerous spending habits?

Some proponents of this recently passed bill argue that billions of dollars from previously passed agreements under Trump's administration will be used for subsidizing this plan. Let us talk reality for a minute: robbing Peter to pay Paul for the sake of a Biden victory on infrastructure doesn't solve the problem of rising inflation, empty shelves, and workers being laid off because of authoritarian mandates.

Government under this administration is spending America into oblivion. We need to reign in the fiscal irresponsibility and overreach of the current administration. Certainly, this bill *marketed* as infrastructure and social good is a rose by another name -higher taxes, forced lifestyles, and an even larger national deficit.

Article I, section 8, clause 1 of our Constitution was intended to give taxing power to Congress for paying off the national debt and to provide for the general welfare, which this administration has broadened the definition of, and is using these moneys for their partisan agendas.

With term limits, we can curtail the overreach of our federal government and restore fiscal responsibility in government spending. The philosophical warfare we are now engaged in is continued spending that creates higher debt and tax burden versus prudence in spending on behalf of a society wishing to flourish.

States Are Standing Up to Federal Tyranny and Hypocrisy

I know no safe depository of the ultimate powers of society but the people themselves; and if we think them not enlightened enough to exercise their control with a wholesome discretion, the remedy is not to take it from them, but to inform their discretion by education.
—Thomas Jefferson

With the same authoritarianism as any other tyrant from ancient times, President Biden is trying to use vaccine mandates to force the American citizenry into undergoing medical procedures against their will. Biden condemned the use of executive orders as dictatorial while campaigning for office but now exemplifies dictatorial leadership like a Roman emperor.

Fortunately, the states are standing in the breach.

A federal judge has temporarily blocked Biden's vaccine mandate after more than two dozen states filed suit against the requirement. American liberties are being challenged daily, but more than three dozen Republican senators have also acted and are intent on removing the authoritarian whip from the Biden administration's grasp. According to a report from Fox News, forty-two Republican senators intend to challenge Biden's controversial vaccine mandate by use of the Congressional Review Act.

Vaccine mandates are not the only thing the states are challenging. Biden's use of the executive order has him facing twenty-one lawsuits from multiple states on matters ranging from the Keystone pipeline, greenhouse gas emissions, and vaccine mandates that threaten personal liberty and the economies of various states. The *Washington Times* reported that the Biden administration is facing lawsuits at a record pace.

James Madison stated:

> "The general government is not to be charged with the whole power of making and administering laws: its jurisdiction is limited to certain enumerated objects, which concern all the members of the republic, but which are not to be attained by the separate provisions of any".

"Enumerated" in government refers to specificity—the Tenth Amendment reminds us that any powers not granted to federal government are reserved to the States, respectively. The greatest existential threat to our constitutional republic is the federal overreach that now exists within it.

The legacy of our forefathers in the form of the Constitution was the breath of life to a new nation. The Constitution was ratified with the strong intention of protecting its citizenry from an oppressive government. The Biden administration is setting a poor example with poor intentions. Mandates that rob the people of their liberties are nothing short of tyranny.

Forty-two Republican senators and two dozen states understand the concept of an overreaching federal government and are making effective use of our constitutional process to rectify it. This is not the government designed by our forefathers, but a government designed by greed, power lust, and enabled by elitists.

If the overreach of this federal government coupled with its hypocritical standards has you concerned about the direction our country is going, there is an opportunity for all of us to be a part of the solution to it.

Article V and the convention of states is the sword of the citizenry that can slash through the overreach of federal government. Some states are standing up for their constituents, but that battle will never end. If Washington has unlimited power under current constitutional interpretation, we the people will never be safe from federal tyranny and hypocrisy. That is why, in their wisdom, our forefathers included Article V within the Constitution. They understood that the time would come when the government would become overreaching and oppressive.

Americans have now crossed into that time.

The problem of federal overreach is the people's opportunity to educate and remind our elected officials that they are the servants, and we are the masters.

In God We Trust, Not Our Representatives

> A body of men holding themselves accountable to
> nobody ought not to be trusted by anybody.
> —Thomas Paine

Let me ask three questions.

- Do you have a firm belief in the reliability of our elected servants?
- Do you have a firm belief that those servants tell us the truth?
- Do you believe firmly in their strength to overcome partisanship and work toward positive effects for all Americans?

If you cannot unequivocally answer yes to these questions, you, my friend, have trust issues with the government, and you should! Here is why.

Let us start with the fiasco at our southern border and immigration. The policy of "give me your tired, your poor" seems to reign supreme on the southern border, while official welcoming to our Canadian friends is not allowed until November 8, 2021 Canadians must be fully vaccinated, but that is not a priority at the southern border. About three in ten encounters of migrants are from other countries. So where exactly are they coming from? Are they vaccinated? Why is the southern border open while the northern is closed until November 8, 2021?

And what is the positive accomplishment of forcing health workers to comply with becoming vaccinated or to lose their job, especially when new data is suggesting that this experimental vaccine has numerous questionable flaws?

The double standard of enforcement and the definition of violence seems to change like the wind depending on how it can serve the overreaching federal government. Parents concerned about the mental and physical health of their children under the stress of forced mask mandates are being threatened with domestic terrorism by their opposition. School boards are asking for federal intervention at meetings because of the so-called escalating violence. It depends on the definition that is applied, doesn't it? Violence for me is unnecessary force. In its application by our current administration, it is defined as any opposition against questionable behavior and bad policy!

We have become all too aware of how the word "insurrection" is being applied to patriots invited into the Capitol on Biden's inauguration day. People are in prison even though they carried no guns nor committed any property damage. They are labeled as insurrectionists for exercising their First Amendment rights!

In Loudoun County, Virginia, Scott Smith was arrested for challenging the school board's policy on allowing students to use whatever bathroom they desired based on gender identity alone. Smith's daughter had been sexually assaulted a few weeks prior, but at the board meeting he was accused of lying. The boy was charged with two counts of forcible sodomy, one count of anal sodomy, and one count of forcible fellatio. Weeks later, while the boy was supposed to be on house arrest, he sexually assaulted another girl after being transferred to another school.

Welcome to Biden's version of Build Back Better, where the Attorney General's office is being weaponized to go after dissenting parents whose only crime is trying to raise their children in safety and exercising the freedom to choose the best policies for doing that!

Now more than ever is the time for a convention of states to be enacted. We the people are the true administrators of self-governance. It is our duty alone to restore trust, integrity, respect, and service within our government.

The question remains: is there enough ambition within our citizenry to counteract the authoritarian ambitions of Marxist ideology running rampant within the business of our government and the government of business?

One mind, one cause, in united effort: this is the philosophical warfare of the commoner.

Federal Overreach and Community Division

The *Federalist Paper* most cited by justices of the Supreme Court is number 78, where Alexander Hamilton said, "The judiciary branch of the proposed government would be the weakest of the three branches because it had no influence over either the sword or the purse".

Supreme Court Justice Sonia Sotomayor was caught pushing lies about the coronavirus to ram through Joe Biden's federal vaccine injections on Americans. Sotomayor claimed, "Over 100,000 children which we've never had before, are in serious condition, many on ventilators." Numerous fact-checkers have proven this claim to be false. In reality, at this time of this writing, there are fewer than 3,500 children in hospitals from coronavirus. CDC Director Rochelle Walensky was forced to come forward and clarify that the number of children hospitalized with COVID-19 was nowhere close to the statistic put forth by Sotomayor. In an interview with Fox News, Walensky also stated that COVID hospitalizations include patients who go to hospitals for other reasons and happen to test positive while they are there. Senator Rand Paul responded to this by asking, "Is Fauci advising Justice Sotomayor?"

Fear tactics and false and hyperbolic language come down from on high, and confirmation bias spreads the lie as a truth.

Here in my own state of Florida, the community I live in has been affected by false narratives of a nefarious agenda and misinformation. The latest weaponization of these similar scare tactics in the community where I live is the arbitrary exclusion of the unvaccinated for a planned Valentine's Day party. The sponsors of this event are forcing all attendees to show proof of experimental vaccination. Isn't it interesting—a celebration of love exclusive to certain members only?

Cancel culture is alive and well in the nation. Even though the policy of our governor reflects inclusivity, there are the factions fueled by the false narratives who take it upon themselves to do otherwise. Like a cancer, a socialist and authoritarian archetype is spreading throughout community life here in the free state of Florida. Many liberty-loving citizens here in Florida are frustrated by the groupthink of cancel culture and virtue signaling. The good news is that when trouble is on your own doorstep, it becomes a call to action.

The battle is much larger than a Valentine's Day celebration. The solution for ridding America of these toxic confederations our forefathers warned us about resides within Article V, a convention of states. The overreach of federal mandates and policy are now falsely encouraging people to think they can enforce unconstitutional policy and behavior.

If it is not clear by now that the policies of this current administration are further dividing Americans and that federal overreach is out of control, then there is none so blind than those who refuse to see! We need amendments to our Constitution and using Article V will bring an end to divisive policies made by the aristocracy residing in our federal government.

CHAPTER 5

Federal Overreach Illuminates State Sovereignty

The problem with bureaucracy within the federal government is that the vision of "We the People" is not often reflected in its policy making. Corporations influence federal policy making with large donations in exchange for whatever serves the corporations' interests.

We have all witnessed the flip-flops of the CDC and are acutely aware of how government-funded agencies reflect the narrative of party agendas rather than considering the other risks involved for healthy living, a flourishing economy, and foremost, our individual freedoms. The good news is that the shadow behavior of our federal government is illuminating individual state sovereignty in doing for its people what the federal government will not. Good leadership within the state government sends a loud and formidable message to check the overreach of the federal machine and reminds us of the revolutionary slogan "Don't Tread on Me!"

Why Is Joe Biden Paying Illegal Immigrants $450,000 Per Child?

> I own I am not a friend to a very energetic
> government. It is always oppressive.
> —Thomas Jefferson

What are the priorities of the Biden administration?

If their latest immigration policy is any indication, it isn't Americans, service people, or their families. The US Departments of Justice, Homeland Security, and Health and Human Services are working in concert with legislators to give $450,000 to each illegal immigrant who was detained and separated from their children under President Donald Trump. That means a family of four could be awarded $1.8 million, a bigger payout than many Gold Star families or the victims of 9/11. Taxpayers will be forced to foot the bill for Biden's generosity—not toward hardworking Americans but for illegal immigrants who have suffered "psychological trauma" from being separated from their children at the border.

While the citizenry of America struggles through oppressive mandates and inflation created by Biden's policies and regulations, illegal immigrants could become millionaires at our expense. Taxation without representation caused a rift between the colonies and Great Britain. King George's tyranny has reemerged through the policy making of our current administration. Americans are being punished for crimes we did not commit, and as an enhancer, we are not asked but forced to pay a monetary premium to the perpetrators. What is framed as "unfair" for illegals (being detained for illegal entry) is not unfair to us (paying reparations).

A government that was designed to work on behalf of its citizenry now punishes those off whose back this country was built on and unfairly wants to make lawbreakers into millionaires. The professional citizenry of America is being asked to take comfort and immense pride in doing without while the overreach of federal government tries to do us in!

The ubiquitous inconsistencies of this present administration are not by accident but designed. Frustration for too long a period could take anyone past the breaking point. Stress comes from frustration, followed by submission. As Thomas Paine stated, "These are the times that try men's souls."

The peaceful way for counteracting oppressive ambitions of federal overreach is through our own improvisation, adaptation, and overcoming lunacy with the reason and intellect of Article V of the Constitution.

Our workforce is being punished for not submitting to unconstitutional mandates and political extortions. In Biden's America, the everyday American is expendable and a political commodity.

Biden's Build Back Better is not inclusive for all Americans. Build Back Better is for keeping the aristocracy in charge through the gratitude and votes of illegal millionaires whose allegiance is bought and paid for.

If history has taught us anything, it is the fact that the commoners become uncommon in their valor when governments become too tyrannical and oppressive.

Our Ships Have Come In

The greatest ability in business is to get along with
others and to influence their actions.
—John Hancock

With federal decisions and mandates negatively impacting the supply chain, it is decisions made in sovereign states by local governments that come to the rescue. Florida chose to be a part of the solution for alleviating the holiday blues in 2021.

Slews of ships from the East Coast were being rerouted to Florida, along with a cargo ship from India, according to an article in *Florida Politics*. Increases in the cost of holiday celebrations were to be expected, but the business of getting along with others and influencing their actions, reflected in the policies of Governor DeSantis, can counteract shortages of supplies for Floridians. As John Adams stated," Every problem is an opportunity in disguise." In Florida, the opportunity in disguise was unmasked just before and during Halloween. Rather than opting for the *trick* of holidays being impacted by short supply, Floridians were *treated* with the benefits of good policy and prompt execution by local government actions.

In his statement to William Penn on July 21, 1816, Thomas Jefferson wrote,

> I, however, place economy among the first and most important republican virtues, and public debt as the greatest of the dangers to be feared.

Does it seem to you, as it does to me, that folks in Florida are in good hands because of leadership regarding the economy? We have an opportunity to reflect here on the benefits of local government having authority over issues impacting a state of constituents versus an overreaching federal government which may not be able to provide the best situation for all states with one policy.

The whole purpose of a convention of states is to ensure sovereignty of states. Article V is the Constitutional battering ram we the people can activate for ensuring that type and quality of servitude among our elected officials.

Through Article V, the citizenry of America can limit or eliminate the shadow government, using new constitutional amendments to restore integrity and accountability in government.

Yes, our ships are coming in and goods are being delivered, but we must stay ever vigilant and stoke the embers of our ambition to pass a convention of states in thirty-four states to reset the field in all areas of overreach. Our goal must be bigger than a 2021 Thanksgiving and Christmas. Our goal is to restore integrity, honesty, and accountability to our republic.

We must always bear in mind that government is our servant—we are its master. That was the vision of our forefathers while they hammered out the details of our Constitution. The intention of guaranteeing that we the people remain master is why Article V exists for us today.

When a Lie Becomes the Truth

Power depends on people creating and believing in fictions. Joseph Goebbels was the media wizard of the Nazi propaganda machine who explained that "a lie told once remains a lie, but a lie told a thousand times becomes the truth."

The shadow of technology is that it can be weaponized for the dissemination of judgments and opinion as hard facts. Narratives easily become mythology generating false beliefs. The fundamental principle of propaganda success is to confine it to only a few points and repeat them over and over. The global elite commands most of the conversation. Everyone else is silenced.

Convention of States Florida volunteers are alchemizing that conundrum. They are helping people change the way they feel by informing the way they think. Convention of States currently has over 160,000 petition signers and new volunteers daily who are eager to spread the truth of Article V of the Constitution.

The ancient Talmud states, "We see the world the way we are, not the way it is." There is abundant evidence that most Floridians see the world the way they believe it can be and do not buy into the mythology of despair, doom, and death. The people who are perishing are those who lack a vision of how they want to live. And yet the hope and message of the Convention of States is changing hearts and changing minds. By reaching, teaching, and activating others, the great state of Florida will have its political legacy and boon to offer sister states beyond sightings of alligators and ospreys and exporting orange juice. Florida is shining as a state because it is fostering positive attitudes through patriotic actions, nurturing growth through knowledge, and affecting outcomes by concentrated efforts and unity.

Sharing these three qualities with others in our work restores the vision of the perishing. Death, doom, and despair is now being replaced with hope, charity, and faith.

Isn't it faith in action that precedes the manifestation of the miraculous?

Encouragement for the Leaders

Florida was the third state to pass the COSA Convention of States resolution and is working in concert with other states to pass this same resolution, which would put an end to federal overreach, force accountability in federal spending, and add term limits for federal offices to the Constitution. We can be proud of our state as an arbiter of restoring sanity to government on both state and federal levels.

As I write, I would like to think the arduous work of COS leaders in Florida and other states have fueled the desire for Wisconsin volunteers to influence their elected servants to adopt this resolution. The Badger State of Wisconsin, like badgers themselves, are showing the appropriate aggression it takes for the needed changes to occur in our federal government. "Forward! Ever forward!" is the motto and battle cry of the Wisconsin patriots. This type of resolve will, I hope, bolster other remaining states to follow their example and insist upon limiting federal overreach, restoring federal fiscal responsibility, and imposing term limits on career politicians.

Slowly we turn, inch by inch, and state by state …

By way of example, Florida is taking the spirit of Thomas Jefferson's quote in literal form: "What country can preserve its liberties if its rulers are not warned from time to time that their people preserve the spirit of resistance? Let them take arms." The "arms" taken up are not the conventional weaponry of military might, but the collective energies of organizing, educating, activating, and adjusting to the tactics of those who work to reduce individual liberties and states' rights.

We are reaching the summit of our uphill climb. We can be encouraged but must remain resolute, reminding ourselves that until the convention is called, there is still much work to be done. But hurray for

COSA! Hurray for the dedicated volunteers in every state still building engaged armies to reach, teach, and activate others in the call to noble action.

Our ambitions must remain indefatigable to counteract those confederations whose purpose is to reduce our liberties while they gorge themselves on personal wealth and power. Leaders are getting it done!

CHAPTER 6

Keeping Our Spirits Alive

Americans today are all living within a season of political consternation. We wonder when the political turmoil will end, or if indeed it will ever end.

We must be ever mindful that as individuals, we each carry personal shadows—those things we hide, repress, and deny. Should we then expect our elected servants to be any different?

Self-governance holds a great cost for apathy, for which we are now paying the price. But the remedy lies in acting, learning, and adapting to what threatens our liberty. It is not too late, as we are closing in on the thirty-four states needed to call for a convention of states.

Negativity and despair looms daily in the media. This is the time for cleaving to the values, attitudes, and beliefs that we have forged from our lifetime of personal world-building. How did any of us succeed where others said we would fail? By keeping our spirits alive!

Federal Lies and Betrayal

> I do solemnly swear (or affirm) that I will faithfully execute the Office of President of the United States, and will to the best of my ability, preserve, protect, and defend the Constitution of the United States.

Immigration decisions are made through constitutional law as the responsibility of Congress. Yet it seems our Commander in Chief has overstepped his authority by using taxpayers' money to bring immigrants into America.

The Vice President's oath of office is as follows:

> I do solemnly swear (or affirm) that I will support and defend the Constitution of the United States against all enemies, foreign and domestic; that I will bear true faith and allegiance to the same; that I take this obligation freely, without any mental reservation or purpose of evasion; that I will well and faithfully discharge the duties of the office on which I am about to enter so help me God.

"Nothing short of betrayal," said a federal government contractor employed to transport migrants from the southern border to the airport. Flights arrive after curfew, and no information is being given to police to prevent the breach of security protocols.

Illegal border crossings are soaring to record levels, and our Commander in Chief is enabling it to its fullest capacity. Currently, there is no substantive plan for putting millions of illegal immigrants on a direct path to citizenship. So, one must wonder, how is this *building back better?* The question that should be on the minds of our elected is, is this an impeachable offense for an abuse of power that subverts the Constitution?

"Shall any man be above justice?" George Mason asked. "Shall that man be above it who can commit the most extensive injustice?"

The American people are being lied to, manipulated, and ripped off by this current administration. To date, twenty-six states have joined in a lawsuit challenging the Biden administration's vaccine mandates for businesses.

The Convention of States Action is gaining ground in the battle for curbing federal overreach, and the remaining tenets of term limits and accountability in spending.

Is impeachment on the forefront? Is Biden's administration subverting the Constitution? There are now twenty-six states contending that he is.

Inflation has reached its highest level since 1982, millions of illegal immigrants flood the country, we faced failure in Afghanistan, and Biden's promise to get COVID under control has not been met. Is this the Biden plan for building back better? If so, America cannot afford it!

Thankfully, the wisdom of our forefathers, along with their deep understanding of human nature, gave them the foresight to add Article V, the convention of states, to the Constitution. Volunteers work day, and night to bring legislators together for the sole purpose of restoring constitutional principles over presidential personalities and personal whims. The narrative pushed onto us is safety by vaccination, but the current data does not support that claim. This administration defines safety by forcing experimental vaccinations onto American, while illegal immigrants flood our borders in a clandestine method.

When the guest list is unlimited, the host is at fault when things get out of hand … and things certainly are!

Epitaph of the Commoner

If we can see, and *if* we can understand and differentiate between right and wrong in today's world of algorithmic manipulations, biased media, fact-checkers, and weaponized science, then we can unite against the common enemy. The epitaph that elitists and the aristocracy would enjoy writing about the American citizenry is

THEY DIED FIGHTING AGAINST THEIR OWN PROJECTIONS
LET US TOAST THE NEW WORLD ORDER AND GREAT
RESET

As a content writer for the state of Florida, I spend much of my time researching data of all types. Men like John Jay, Alexander Hamilton, and James Madison, who authored the *Federalist Papers* that eventually helped the ratification process of the Constitution, often warned against the nature of humankind in life and government. We see the shadow nature of elected servants inflating to the point of producing bad policy making through party agenda loyalties while disregarding their loyalty and oath to constitutional law.

The general welfare clause has been weaponized by making private businesses "nonessential" and forcing mandates of masks and vaccinations, causing people to move from one state to another. This overreach of federal government lends the opportunity for another epitaph that can be written for the commoner:

LIBERTY AND FREEDOM ARE NOT DIFFICULT TO STEAL
FROM THE COMMONER
WHEN THE NARRATIVE OF SAFETY, AND COMMON
WELFARE FOR THE CITIZENRY
IS BEING EXPLOITED

We are being gaslighted by many of our federal leaders. Cancel culture, in the nefarious paradigm of multiculturalism, is the agent of aggression toward those who hold different world views and political ideologies. Enumerated powers do not allow the federal government to pass mandates that give our elected officials the throne of being society's moral arbiters!

The love of money and power was a topic that our forefathers often wrestled with. While wordsmithing the draft of our Constitution, they were highly concerned with "bridling" these vices and temptations.

If the citizenry does not insist on an article 5 convention of states intervention, our final epitaph we write for ourselves may be:

WE TRUSTED TOO MUCH WITHOUT VERIFYING,
AND DEARLY PAID THE PRICE!

I have offered my opinion concerning the overreach of our federal government and the efforts made by it for limiting our life, liberty, and pursuit of happiness. I have articulated the insights and intentions set by our wise forefathers, and their ideas of what good government should be. Finally, I have offered a viable solution for solving the problems our government creates by enacting a convention of states as prescribed by Article V.

With united effort and the proper tactics, we can easily replace their epitaphs for us with our own:

WE IMPROVISED, WE ADAPTED, AND WE OVERCAME!

Dakota Windancer

The Federal Government's Sham of Safety

The second leading cause of death among those 10–34 years of age is suicide. Let that sink in.

The first leading cause of death within that same age group is unintentional injury and homicide.

The American Psychology Association has announced that a significant rise in "deaths of despair," resulting from our diminishing social and economic climate. Authoritarian government has placed the citizenry in an ever-constant state of ambiguity and disorientation since the pandemic was declared on March 11, 2020. Psychologists know that when people are kept in this state long enough, they will break down mentally, leading to anxiety, depression, and suicidal ideation.

What is especially heinous in our federal government's action is that the current narrative, gamed on the American people by our current administration and media, is "We are concerned for the general welfare and safety of all Americans." The American citizen has become a character in the fairytale of Hansel and Gretel, who are abandoned in the forest wandering hungry, and confused. Finally, the two fall into the hands of a witch who lives in a house made of gingerbread, cake, and candy. Is it prudent to trust the witch who attracts us with cake and candy ("free" healthcare, "free" college tuition)? Should the government takeover, what should be familial decisions?

Everyone would agree there is much that needs fixing in our federal government—of that there can be no doubt. For a moment, let us set aside the issue of the efficacy of the COVID-19 vaccine. Violent crime is on the rise in every major city. Could this be a consequence of the despair and the social and economic decline now taking place? How exactly is our current administration addressing that? Supposedly, disarming the American people will make the bad guys go away.

Like a tough beef roast in a pressure cooker, we the people are being "cooked," and we do not know how long this will last. It is the year of 2021 and children are drawing pictures of themselves in school with eyes only because mask mandates are diminishing their identities. This war on American society, and the world, is being carefully orchestrated by the elitists whose mantra is "It is good for thee, but not for me."

There are no enumerated powers that give Congress or the president the right to force the citizenry, much less the states, into compliance with their definitions of health. A vital component of self-governance is taking personal responsibility in affairs of government even to the point of civil disobedience, especially when it comes to our physical and mental health. As clinical psychologist Jordan Peterson has stated, "Men and women must become dangerous again. Dangerous—because that connotes formidability." I suspect there are many Americans who, like me, would rather enjoy the freedom that is obtained by the willingness to take risks. They are ready to assume the responsibilities that come with it.

Like Hansel and Gretel, we must learn to discern the trappings that confound our choice of survival. Too many sweets can cause diabetes, just as too many giveaways cause codependence on the government. Fairy tales were written to illuminate human psychology. This is not a fairytale, folks, but we can learn from it. Survival depends on a good balance of personal responsibility and support from other sources.

A Visit from the Christmas Spirit

'Twas the night before Christmas, and the senators got
    soused;
They were anxious about who would remain in the
    House.
The stock markets clung to a hope and a prayer,
But so far in Florida our shelves are not bare.
The opt-out policy saved children from masks,
And COS servants helped achieve that task!
What will come next and be dropped in our lap?
Whatever it is, COS won't be taking a nap!
Amidst all the rancor, spittle, and chatter,
COS provides a solution as big as the matter.
Away to the halls of Congress we fly like a flash,
Ridding our government of unwanted trash.
A momentous day's coming when government will flow
Giving voice to its people who were made to bend low.
When what to our wondering eyes should appear—
Well, not a sleigh and eight tiny reindeer.
Adapting, adjusting, and learning is the trick
To enact a convention, and hopefully quick!
"Now, Abbott! Now, Levin! Now, Meckler and Rubin!
On, Green! On, Paul! On DeSantis and Palin!
To the top of the heap, to the top of the Wall,
Now dash away! Dash away! Dash away all!"
As leaves that before the wild hurricane fly
When they meet with an obstacle, mount to the sky.
So up to the White House the courses they flew,
With limits for fed terms, spending, and overreach too!
With a twinkle in the eye and a hymn in the heart,
We work for future glory of what we give start.
Men and women together are unanimous in cause.

In fervor we work to rescind authoritarian laws.
Block-walking and writing, webinars, and meetings—
At the Tallahassee rally we share our greetings.
COS works on behalf of children for the day

Saved from experimental vaccines and masks as they play.

Christmas reminds us of the blessings in life:
food, shelter, clothing, a husband, or wife.
Take time and give inventory to the value of your life.
Put more energy into loving than you do into strife.
While some may say, "I'll believe it when I see it,"
Volunteers know if we believe it, we'll achieve it!
As this year draws to its close and is soon out of sight,
I bid Merry Christmas to all, and to all a good night!

Epilogue

It has been said that "war is when the government tells you who the bad guy is. Revolution is when you decide that for yourself."

Benjamin Franklin provided a formula for remedying those things we wish to change: "Energy and persistence conquer all things."

We are at the critical point of retaining a government made by the people, for the people. We are engaged in not only a cultural revolution but also a political revolution that may determine whether we remain a constitutional republic or become a socialist/communist regime.

The nature of the world is that wherever there is chaos, there is also order. We live in a time when we are inundated with "metaverse" reality and artificial intelligence bolstered by fake news and social media censorship. Media that enables our current administration has become a modern-day false prophet, calling us to worship the god of government. This worship of government is the world and the type of shadow government our forefathers warned us about!

We stand face to face with a government that projects its collective shadows upon American society, asking the citizenry to change who they are for their self-serving agendas. But the role of the federal government is limited by the enumerated powers within the Constitution.

In the natural world, the big fish eat the little fish very easily when they are separated from the school. An amazing thing happens when the school remains intact and acts as one collective agent that confuses the predator with its "collective mind of movement" and eliminates the threat of consumption by the larger fish.

That is the point of this book: "a collective mind of movement." If we wish to eliminate the threat of a predatory government whose aim is to disempower the citizenry, we must act with a collective mind of movement. A convention of states would eliminate the threat of federal overreach, restore fiscal responsibility by adding a balanced budget amendment, and impose term limits on our federal representatives. Doing these things will make it much more difficult for them to create private confederations among themselves—which our forefathers also warned about—that do not serve the best interests of the people.

You and I must decide what type of government we want not only for ourselves but for future generations. We need to teach our children that inalienable rights are nonnegotiable and that they have a divine right to life, liberty, and the pursuit of happiness. We must keep our spirits alive by activating the spirit and intent of government held for us in the preamble of the US Constitution:

> We the People of the United States, in order to form as more perfect Union, establish Justice, ensure domestic Tranquility, provide for the common defense, promote the general Welfare, and secure the Blessings of Liberty to ourselves and our Posterity, do ordain and establish this Constitution for the United States of America.

It is and always has been the nature of man to subvert order for personal gain. Ironically, it has also always been the nature of man to alchemize order from chaos.

The philosophical warfare we now find ourselves engaged in is not about political party or race, religion, and gender—these are the smokescreens of the aristocracy used effectively in dividing the commoners into waging war against themselves, unaware that the true enemy, aristocracy, is pulling the strings!

The ancient Talmud states: "We see the world the way we are, not the way it is." We can be grateful that the worldview of our forefathers was rooted in the document of the Constitution with a sovereign spirit of nurturing, fostering, and affecting the very best of outcomes for all Americans.

It is up to us, the commoners, to embrace that same vision and keep its spirit alive and fix what is wrong in our government. America will either shine as a beacon in a darkening world or become a fairytale of what once was.